ALSO BY LOUIS JENKINS

TIN FLAG

TIN FLAG

NEW AND SELECTED PROSE POEMS

Including all poems from NICE FISH, the play

LOUIS JENKINS

Will o' the Wisp Books

Published by Will o' the Wisp Books 2013

Printed in Canada

Cover art: James G. Davis, *The White Cow*, oil on canvas, 77" x 65" 1987 © James G. Davis
Cover design by Amy Jenkins

ISBN 978-0-9793128-4-7

Will o' the Wisp Books
Duluth, Minnesota
www.willothewispbooks.com

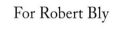

For Robert Bly

TABLE OF CONTENTS
NEW AND SELECTED PROSE POEMS

POEMS FROM THE PLAY NICE FISH

The Discovered Country

Watching a performance of the play "Nice Fish," recently at the Guthrie Theatre, I realized that Louis Jenkins has long been a writer of soliloquies. (Am I the last person to get this?)

I keep my clothes in a suitcase at the foot of my bed. I haven't been anywhere and have no plans to go anywhere, but these days you never know...

Or sometimes a Jenkins poem may resemble the voice-over in a French movie, or the cordial voice of the narrator in a film about, say, a small town that was just missed by a wayward meteorite, or a documentary about bears, maybe a collaboration between Woody Allen and Werner Herzog...

In those days he could fit everything he owned into the back of his Volkswagen, but the fish changed all that.

When David Byrne, another soliloquist, sings about peering down on America from an airplane into the lives of the people on the ground below, and declares "I wouldn't live there if you paid me," we agree wholeheartedly.

They used newspaper for toilet tissue, newspaper for chinking between the logs, the words carefully mouthed and puzzled over then shoved into a crack. Once a month someone made the long trip into town to sell the eggs and buy a newspaper.

Nevertheless, we do live there. Louis Jenkins' prose

poems document what we have to say, acting out, in the roles of ourselves, our arguments with that barely improbable world (and the thousand natural shocks that flesh is heir to) as we walk around steered by the dopey logic of idiom, providing sport for our neighbors.

Because of my extraordinary political correctness and sensitivity of late, I have been elevated to the status of Temporary Minor Saint (secular)...I move about at a slow and stately speed as befits my new rank.
So just who are the speakers in these poems, these debugging patches for one's personal software? More often now than in his earlier work it is the author himself, or more precisely, one of his avatars.

It turns out that everything I've written is untrue.
But it's also sometimes me. Or you.

Phil Dentinger

NEW AND SELECTED PROSE POEMS

MAILBOXES

Some are brightly painted and large as if anticipating great packages. Most are smaller, gray and dented with rust spots; some held together with rope or duct tape, having been slapped more than once by the snow plow. Still they seem hopeful . . . perhaps a Village Shopper or a credit card offer. . . . Once in awhile one raises a modest tin flag. "I have something. It isn't much. I'd like you to take it." All along Highway 2, on Hunter Road and Dahl Road, past Cane Lake, past the gravel pit, and the last refrigerator shot full of holes and dumped into the swamp, mailboxes reach out on extended arms, all the way to the end of the route where balsam and spruce crowd together in the ditches, reaching out. . . .

BASEMENT

There's something about our basement that causes forgetting. I go down for something, say a roll of paper towels, which we keep in a big box down there, and as soon as I get to the bottom of the stairs I have forgotten what I came down there for. It happens to my wife as well. So recently we have taken to working in tandem like spelunkers. One of us stands at the top of the stairs while the other descends. When the descendant has reached the bottom stair, the person at the top calls out, "Light bulbs, 60 watt." This usually works unless the one in the basement lingers too long. I blame this memory loss on all the stuff in the basement. Too much baggage: 10 shades of blue paint, because we could not get the right color, extra dishes, bicycles, the washer and dryer, a cider press, a piano, jars of screws, nails and bolts…. It boggles the mind. My wife blames it on radon.

SIT DOWN

I often spend a good portion of each day trying to find the right place to sit down. The place you choose to sit must be the right height, not too low because of the difficulty of rising again. An Adirondack chair is a bad choice, as is a canoe. I know of two or three rocks along the shore of Lake Superior that I find to be of a comfortable height and good for a short stay; hardness is another factor. Sofas are usually a bad choice, especially if it's your girlfriend's parent's sofa. Don't sit on the edge of a bed. Chairs in the dentist's office waiting room are always uncomfortable. Actually, an overturned bucket overlooking a hole in the ice is probably better, but not by much.

On a sunny day in late March or early April you can get yourself a good sturdy straight-backed chair and go to the south side of the shack, sit down and lean back, chair and all, against the sun-warmed tarpaper wall. You've got the back legs of the chair planted in the snow for extra support. You can just doze there, while the sunlight soaks into the black paper-covered wall, and into you, and you soak into the black background, deeper and deeper until you disappear.

LIFE IN THE WOODS

The woods around you have grown up sheerly to depress you with their dampness and dark. The small birds have all flown away, leaving you alone in the gloom. For a point of reference there's a pile of rusted cans and broken bottles. For company there are mosquitoes. If you call out for help you are put on hold.

If you live long enough in the forest, the forest people, some so old and bent over that their long noses touch the ground, the hidden ones, those conversant with the moon and the devil and the west wind, may come in the night once or twice a month and clean your bathroom. Or not. Which means they don't like you.

HAIRCUT

Shall I wait to get my haircut after my hair has gotten too long, have it cut too short and await the day, the hour, when my hair reaches its perfect length? Or should I have it cut often, keeping my coif constantly at its optimum length? That becomes expensive and besides I like to live in anticipation of the moment. But the moment passes so quickly. For instance, there must have been a period in my life when I was at my peak. Maybe it was only a year or so when, at last, I got my act together, maybe for only a few weeks, or days, when my mental and physical powers were at their fullest. Maybe it was only a couple of hours in the early morning of some forgotten day and I slept through the whole thing. And when I woke, things had begun to deteriorate.

MARCH

It hadn't occurred to me until someone at work brought it to my attention that this winter has been going on for eleven years. I said, "That can't be. Surely not." But then I got thinking about it. It was eleven years ago November we moved into this house. You remember, snow was just beginning and we had so much trouble getting the refrigerator down the driveway and through the door. Danny was eight and we got him a sled for Christmas. It's amazing how one gets concerned with other things and the time just goes by. Here it is March and now that I've noticed it, the snow has begun to melt a little. During the day there's water running in the street. It's like a bird singing in a tree that flies just as you become aware of it. When you think about it, the world, cold and hard as it is, begins to fall apart.

I SAW MAMA KISSING SANTA CLAUS

What neither junior nor his father knows is that she sees him every time he phones. The off-season, mostly. So it isn't true that Santa only comes once a year. She does her hair, her makeup, and puts on the little black dress he likes so much, and her heels. She goes to meet him in some little out-of-the-way joint downtown. It's difficult for a high-profile guy like Santa to be discreet. What does she see in him anyway? Overweight and god knows how old, red-faced, slack-jawed and snoring now in room 308 of the Seafarer's Hotel? Well, it's true, he can be fun, his humor and generosity are legendary. But she sees this can't last. Perhaps though, despite her slight feeling of disappointment and the obvious impossibility of the whole affair, she still holds out some faint hope. A belief in something wondrous about to happen, that somehow this year will be better than last.

AWAKE AT NIGHT

They lie awake for an hour or more, motionless, neither speaking, under their covers making a shape like two low hills or like two long gray clouds that roll in on an afternoon in late fall. Perhaps they will lie like this, side by side, after death, silent until she says, "What time is it?" And he says, "2093."

Maybe she wants to talk. She says, "I'm having a lot of trouble with Photoshop." And he says, "I don't want to talk about software right now." She snuggles close and says, "Do you want to talk about hardware then?"

MAGNUM OPUS

Back then, I wrote all the time, I wrote like a madman, and I was, of course, alone in my dingy little apartment with the nearby freight trains rattling the windows all night long, accentuating my loneliness. It was love, unrequited passion. Nowadays, my ardor cooled somewhat by the years, I write down lines on little scraps of paper and if I come across them, weeks or months, maybe even years later, (the way time goes) they may become part of the magnum opus, or maybe not. I can foresee the time when I will cease to bother with paper and pencils, a more eco-friendly method, and just formulate and arrange the words in my head. And then, later maybe, not even that. Perhaps then the thoughts, the unformed notions will arrive and pass by like birds or wisps of clouds, leaving the sky clear and blue.

STARRY STARRY NIGHT

A bazillion stars overhead, and I look up as amazed and baffled as the first hominid who gazed upward must have been, stars passing overhead like a very slow moving flock of birds, going somewhere, disappearing into the wee hours of the morning. I used to be able to recognize some of the constellations, the Pleiades, the Big Dipper, but I have forgotten most. Still, mankind has learned a lot about the cosmos since Galileo's time. A friend of mine said, "My wife bought me a telescope for my birthday, a nice one, very powerful, I've got it set up on the deck. You know, when you look at a star with your naked eye all you see is a little white dot, but when you look at it through a telescope you see a bigger white dot."

OLD WIRING

It is ridiculous to worry about the next world when you can't even do much about this one. I worry about global climate change, about Yellowstone exploding, cosmic debris hitting the earth. I have worried about nuclear weapons in Iran and North Korea until I was just about to doze off. But there is something else, something else… some darkness lurking always nearby …. Then I remember that tangle of wiring in the attic that dates back to the nineteen-twenties, a potential fire-hazard, for sure. I should hire an electrician, but that would be so expensive … I think I'll just let the nameless dread roost there for a while in that nest of wires, while I go for a whiskey, down at the old *Knob and Tube*.

THE PERSONAL HISTORY CHANNEL

For a few dollars more a month you can add the Personal History Channel to your cable package. You can then while away the hours, reviewing the stupid and embarrassing things you did in years gone by. It can be fascinating watching yourself learning to ride a bicycle or going on your first date. When you come to more recent times, however, there are more and more shows that feature you sitting on the couch, eating chips and watching the Personal History Channel.

IN LESS THAN TEN MINUTES

You have to loosen a bolt that's stuck and does not want to budge, God knows why. It was torqued to specs with the finest tools. It is a very delicate operation, the bolt must not be broken. In order to do this you have to work standing on your head. And because of that your white tie drops down into your spaghetti sauce and you break a button that holds up your pants and in less than ten minutes the King of Bhutan is going to present you with an award. Well, you can tie up your pants with the cord that you wear around your neck that holds your ID card, which will then dangle between your legs, and you can paint your tie with more sauce so that it will appear that you have very bad taste, rather than being merely clumsy.... This is the kind of thing we like to do.

PARADISE

January finally drags into February and one fumbles with numb fingers at the ordinary knots and hooks of life. People are irritable, difficult. Some days you want to stay in bed with the covers over your head and dream of paradise. A place where the warm sea washes the white sand. There are a few palm trees on the higher ground, many brightly colored fish in the lagoon, waves breaking on the reef farther out. No one in sight. Occasionally an incredibly large, split-second shark darkens the clear water. Sea birds ride the wind currents, albatross, kittiwake … and pass on. Day after day, sea wind and perfect sky …. You make a big heap of driftwood on the beach.

RASPBERRY RHUBARB PIE

Ann has just taken one of her famous pies from the oven, and the crust has separated all around the perimeter so that the hot filling bubbles up, like lava from a Hawaiian volcano. It is very hot. The crust of the pie floats on the hot filling the way the earth's surface floats on its core of molten magma. Perhaps the center of the earth is hot raspberry-rhubarb filling, but you can't have any, it is much too hot. You are going to have to wait a very long time before you can have any.

SANDALS

I never really feel comfortable wearing sandals. They don't seem right for this northern climate. Up here we are always expecting it to turn cold. We never go anywhere without a jacket. So when it gets warm enough to wear sandals, usually four or five days in early August, it feels as though I'm taking a big risk to do so. Sandals make me realize how vulnerable I am, nothing at all to protect my toes from falling rocks or scalding hot water. If you wear sandals your feet are available to mosquitoes and wood ticks and other vermin. You don't want to walk into the woods wearing sandals; you don't want to play soccer or rugby. I feel more at ease in boots and wool socks, but every summer I wear my sandals once or twice as an indicator that I'm not planning to do anything at all.

OUT OF IT

I'm out of it these days. I guess I have less interest in keeping up to date on what's happening. I don't know the names of most of the current movie stars and have not seen their movies. Same for the music scene. I have not read what everyone is reading. I don't know what's on TV. I'm out of it, but not too far out. I figure somewhere between 12 to 18 inches. I've noticed that when someone speaks to me he or she seems to be addressing a space just a little to my right or left. When it first happened I thought my acquaintance was speaking to someone else. I looked around but there was no one else there. I've tried moving to adjust the conversational direction but the speaker only readjusts. I realized that if I kept moving our conversation would be going in concentric circles. So now I just stand still and let the talk continue at cross-purposes. It is getting worse. Sometimes I can't make any sense at all of what someone is saying, as if he were speaking Welsh, Then I remember that I am in Wales and he is speaking Welsh.

REGRET

There's no use in regret. You can't change anything. Your mother died unhappy with the way you turned out. You and your father were not on speaking terms when he died, and you left your wife for no good reason. Well, it's past. You may as well regret missing out on the conquest of Mexico. That would have been just your kind of thing back when you were eighteen: a bunch of murderous Spaniards, out to destroy a culture and get rich. On the other hand, the Aztecs were no great shakes either. It's hard to know whom to root for in this situation. The Aztecs thought they had to sacrifice lots of people to keep the sun coming up every day. And it worked. The sun rose every day. But it was backbreaking labor, all that sacrificing. The priests had to call in the royal family to help, and their neighbors, the gardener, the cooks.... You can see how this is going to end. You are going to have your bloody, beating heart ripped out, but you are going to have to stand in line, in the hot sun, for hours, waiting your turn.

SMALL FISH

He's too small to keep so I remove the hook and put
him back in the water. He hesitates a moment near
the surface, as if not quite realizing where he is, then
with a swift movement of the tail he's gone. He's
back in it now, his own deep blue-green, the daily
hunger and panic. He has no way of thinking about
this experience. He was, then he was not, and now
he is again. A seizure. But then, moments later, he's
back on the surface a few feet from the boat, lying
on his side, the gills working, one in the water, one in
the useless air. He'd hit the bait hard and the hook
had gone in deep--youthful folly, you could say, or
extreme hunger, or plain bad luck. I reach out and
try to grab him, but he's still too quick even in this
condition. He swims down again. He's determined
but the water will not have him any more. In a
few seconds he's back, farther from the boat, in the
domain of sunlight and hungry seagulls.

FEVER

I am being interviewed for the job of Area Representative. I am flying over the tundra at 250 mph, my nose and fingertips not more than three inches above the ice.

I wake to discover that the glasses and bottles on the table by the bed have crowded together, waiting to be taken across the river.

A pen with an extremely fine point is signing on a tiny scrap of paper my name over and over again. It is all perfectly clear.

I have never really noticed the things in this room. I have been unaware of their articulations: the longings of the chest; the desires of the bed; the faint groaning of the walls at night; those obscure concessions the house makes to the earth, settling.

The room is quiet now, everything falling at the same rate of speed.

ZUCCHINI

You always miss one, and the one overlooked, hidden behind one of the large leaves, grows to an enormous size. These things are best when they are small. You can't give this monster away. You say, "It will make great zucchini bread." "Hmmm, no thanks." What to do? Here you are, responsible for an overweight vegetable. This is not what you had in mind when you planted the seeds. But you can't just throw it away. It looks like you will have to make zucchini bread, even though you don't much like zucchini bread. Perhaps you could give away the zucchini bread after you've made it. On the other hand, you could put the zucchini into a nice basket, along with some carrots and onions or some flowers, place it on someone's porch, ring the door bell and run away.

SUITCASE

I keep my clothes in a suitcase at the foot of my bed. I haven't been anywhere and have no plans to go anywhere, but these days you never know, and besides it gives me a focus for my anxiety and for my occasional moments of unfounded excitement and anticipation. Every morning I take out clean socks and underwear, etcetera, and throw the dirty clothes back in the suitcase. Once a week or so I take the suitcase down to the washer and dryer in the basement and sit around naked waiting for my clean clothes. That's about it. The days pass quickly enough. Once in awhile I see old friends. "You look tired," they say or "Why the long face?" I reply, "Well, you know, it's stressful, living out of a suitcase."

THE WEDDING

"Where is the wedding? What time does it start?"
"I don't know. What did you do with the invitation?
What shall I wear?" Someone said it was at St. Paul's.
Then someone else said that at the last minute the
couple decided to fly to Las Vegas and get married at
a drive-up chapel. Never mind. It's the ideal wedding,
the ideal couple.

Turns out we've missed the ceremony. As we arrive,
the minister is walking away from the church carrying
his robes over his arm. It was hotter than usual today.
He is smiling slightly as he walks, thinking of the
newlyweds, thinking of a gin and tonic.

The old folks have gathered on the church lawn to
chat. Summer hats, white shoes, pink dresses, powder
blue sport coats. "Who was the bride?" No one is sure.
The granddaughter of a friend? A distant cousin's
niece? "But wasn't the bride beautiful?" "And the
groom, so handsome—well, everyone says he's smart,
has a very important job.

Meanwhile the bride and groom have gone to the rose
garden to be photographed. Clouds are gathering in
the west. Thunderstorms are predicted. It makes us
unreasonably happy to see the bride and groom in
their silly outfits, smiling at the camera, the air full of
threat and promise, the smell of rain and of roses.

TANGO

In a relationship like this there is one who does not really care, and that forces the other into the position of the one who does: positive and negative forces, so that things will go around. A tango. The long summer evening, the music … "Why do you treat me this way?" she asks. "I love you, of course …" "I hate you," she says. He takes her hand and pulls her close. "Be careful … my husband … He has a pistol." He doesn't. She made that up. They are careful of the steps, the turns. It is complicated and they are intense, breathless … the other dancers close by. But it is night that is important, the breeze is warm in the beckoning aspen grove where there are lovely grassy clearings. The stars are appearing one by one, and the moon is a mere beginning over the lake, a sliver in the indigo sky.

When the music ends he says, "Thank you, my dear." And she says, "Oh no, thank *you!*"

EXERCISE

Here is a Zen-inspired exercise for all you older guys. Dress comfortably in your shorts and a tee-shirt, hold your trousers in front of you with both hands. You will need to bend forward somewhat in order to hold your pants at knee level or below. Then while balancing on your right leg, lift your left leg and insert it into the left pant leg. Repeat this process lifting your right and balancing on your left leg. See if you can do this without tipping over. Practice without using a chair or other support. This exercise is best done quickly and without thought. But, of course, now you have thought about it.

CONFUSING FALL WARBLERS

This is the way things go: not high and direct like
the geese with all their honking fanfare, or the eagle
riding the rising air, but like the small birds feeding,
moving from bush to tree to weed, with what seems
like no plan at all, just one thing leading to another.

STORIES YOU TELL

There are worse things than being a human being, I suppose. You could be a politician, for instance. The only compensation for being human is that you can make up a good story. But good stories require a good audience, one that is patient and quiet. You could try telling a story to a cow. You'd want to gear the story to your audience. "Once upon a time I walked over by the fence and I stood there for a long time, chewing, looking out across the road … then suddenly PLOP, I dropped a big cow pie. Ha ha ha ha!" The cow just stares at you, chewing. It's no good with dogs either, dogs listen, often with great enthusiasm, but they don't really get it. No good with cats or monkeys. That means you are pretty much stuck with other human beings as your audience. You spend a lifetime getting the stories just right and then you begin: "Once upon a time I walked over by the fence …" and the listener stares into space, chewing, wondering vaguely how long this will last.

THE TENT

Concave on the windward side, convex on the lee, it snaps and strains the ropes. Green nylon not quite the color of the forest, it is the flag of nothing in particular, a banner that proclaims we will not be here very long, a modest shelter shedding only the lightest rains. Like home anywhere, pitched on an unsheltered point, the tent wants to fly into the air, heave sideways into the lake.

THE LONG WINTER

The winter here is so long that one needs to find an outdoor activity to pass the time. Some people ski or snowboard. There's snowmobiling, ice skating, hockey. . . . I prefer ice fishing, Standing around in the cold wind all day, pulling ice fish from a hole in the ice. Ice fish have to be eaten raw, like sushi. If you cook an ice fish you wind up with nothing but a skillet full of water. Gnash one down or swallow it whole, there is nothing like the flavor, full of the glittering, bitter cold of a January day. Your teeth crack, your tongue goes numb, your lips turn blue and your eyes roll back in your head. "God!" you say, "God that was good! Let me have just one more."

BUCKET OF BOLTS

My grandpa had the first car in town, a 1904 Auburn. When the car developed engine trouble and stopped running, there was no one in town who could fix it. So they pushed the car into the blacksmith shop and carefully removed the engine and put each bolt they removed into a bucket. Then they crated up the engine and shipped it, by train, back to the manufacturer in Indiana. In a few weeks the crate came back with a note that the engine had been repaired at no cost to the owner. The problem now was that no one could remember how to put the engine back in the car. There was much discussion, everyone had a theory; the barber, the druggist, even the minister had a few thoughts. Finally the project had to be abandoned. The car never ran again but the engine sat in its crate in the blacksmith shop for years. People went on to other things, births, deaths, new cars…. But a thing like that can persist beyond a lifetime, or two, beyond any memory of its existence, lying in a field somewhere with weeds growing up around it. You could stumble over it if you aren't careful.

I MUST SAY

Now that we have come so far together, so much water gone under the bridge, and now that the shadows lengthen around us, I feel that I must say some things that are difficult for me to say. . . . This is a world of plague-bearing prairie dogs and freshly fried flesh. Where is the fish sauce shop, and when did the Irish wristwatch shop shut? Are our oars oak? Are the sheep asleep in the shed? I cannot give you specific statistics but surely the sun will shine soon. Surely the sun will shine on the stop signs and on the twin-screw steel cruisers.

I have lain awake nights thinking of how to say this. I can only hope that what these words lack in meaning will be somehow compensated for by your understanding of my need to say them, and by your knowing that these words are meant for you. Though who you are in this context is never made clear, and it is quite possible that you, yourself, do not know.

BASSOON

The very slightest of winds moves the curtains, the violins faint tremolo just before dawn. Then you hear again the voice you know so well, a voice at once your own and not your own, a voice that may have gone on all night long and, for all you know, may continue long after your eyes have closed. The sound of a bassoon perhaps, that stumbles like a bumblebee from flower to brick wall to water bucket, yet is clear and sweet in the early light before the full cacophony of the day begins. Birdsong. Children's voices - flutes and piccolos, quick, high-pitched and somewhat annoying. "Oh, Grandpa," they say, "not another one of your long, boring stories!"

LATE OCTOBER ABOVE LAKE SUPERIOR

A north wind shakes the last few yellow leaves clinging to a thin popple tree. It's easy to tell what's coming. Old leaves must fall to make way for the new. That's all well and good as long as it's not your turn to go. Keep the dead waiting! Keep the unborn waiting! There's not much to this life anyway, some notions, some longings that come and go like the sea, like sun and shadow played across the stone. This weather is not so bad if you can find a place among the rocks out of the wind.

BREAKFAST

Now that the fun is over maybe it is time to take yourself away to a hermitage high in the mountains, to become a contemplative. But one doesn't want to rush into something like that. It's difficult. Once we stayed out all night drinking under the summer stars and at two AM someone said, "Let's drive to Aspen." "Great idea!" We don't do that anymore. What's left then? I think, breakfast. Perhaps a bowl of oatmeal, with raisins, or a soft-boiled egg…. The sun is shining; a touch of fall in the air, and coffee is ready. The other morning some old friends called, people I haven't seen in 50 years, people with whom I have nothing in common. "We just got married! We're in town, on our honeymoon!" Ridiculous. "Well hell," I said. "Come on over, we'll have some coffee, some bacon and eggs. We'll talk about protein and carbohydrates. We'll talk about distance and speed and gas mileage."

POEMS FROM THE PLAY NICE FISH

THE ICE FISHERMAN

From here he appears as a black spot, one of the shadows that today has found it necessary to assume solid form, and along with the black jut of shoreline far to the left, is the only break in the undifferentiated gray of ice and overcast sky. Here is a man going jiggidy-jig-jig in a black hole. Depth and the current are of only incidental interest to him. He's after something big, something down there that is pure need, something that, had it the wherewithal, would swallow him whole. Right now nothing is happening. The fisherman stands and straightens, back to the wind. He stays out on the ice all day.

THE FISHING LURE

I've spent a great deal of my life fretting over things that most people wouldn't waste their time on. Trying to explain things I haven't a clue about. It's given me that worried look, that wide-eyed, staring look. The look that wild animals sometimes have, deer for instance, standing in the middle of the highway trying to make sense of the situation: "What is that?" Motionless, transfixed. The same look that's on the face of the fishing lure. Stupidity? Terror? What is the right bait for these conditions? High cirrus clouds, cold front moving in. It's all a trick anyway. What is this thing supposed to be? A minnow? A bug? Gaudy paint and hooks all over. It's like bleached blond hair and bright red lipstick. Nobody really believes it. There isn't a way in the world I'd bite on that thing. But I might swim in just a little closer.

THE BACK COUNTRY

When you are in town, wearing some kind of uniform is helpful, policeman, priest, etc. Driving a tank is very impressive, or a car with official lettering on the side. If that isn't to your taste, you could join the revolution, wear an armband, carry a homemade flag tied to a broom handle, or a placard bearing an incendiary slogan. At the very least you should wear a suit and carry a briefcase and a cell phone, or wear a team jacket and a baseball cap and carry a cell phone. If you go into the woods, the back country, someplace past all human habitation, it is a good idea to wear orange and carry a gun, or, depending on the season, carry a fishing pole, or a camera with a big lens. Otherwise, it might appear that you have no idea what you are doing, that you are merely wandering the earth, no particular reason for being here, no particular place to go.

WRISTWATCH

In the morning, after I dressed, I looked for my wristwatch on the nightstand and discovered that it was missing. I looked in the drawer and on the floor, under the bed. It was nowhere to be seen. I looked in the bathroom, checked the pockets of my jacket, my pants. I looked downstairs in the kitchen, the living room. I went out to check the car. I went to the basement and looked through the laundry. I went back upstairs and looked everywhere again. I said, "Have you seen my watch?" to my wife, my children. "I'm sure I left it on the nightstand." I became obsessed with finding the watch. I removed all the drawers from the dresser one by one, emptying their contents onto the bedroom floor. Impossible. Someone must have come in the night and taken it. A watch thief, who with great stealth and cunning, disdaining silverware, jewelry, cameras, fine art, money, had made his way to the bedside and stolen my Timex wristwatch. Perhaps my wife has, for years, been harboring some secret grudge and finally, unable to bear it any longer, took revenge by flushing my watch down the toilet. Maybe my seven-year-old is supporting a drug habit. One thing is certain: nothing, nothing was the way I thought it was.

IF IT WAS A SNAKE

You've lost something, your car keys, or your watch and you have searched for what seems like hours. But then suddenly it appears, right there on the table, not two feet away. "If it was a snake it would have bit you," Mother said. That's what you remember, a phrase, an old saying. My sister said, "Grandma told me, 'Never wear horizontal stripes, they make you look fat.' That's one of the few things I remember about Grandma." Or the words disappear and an image remains. I was getting a lecture from my parents about riding my tricycle all the way downtown. I don't remember anything they said. I remember looking out the window, it was just dark, and a block away a man wearing a white shirt and a tie passed under the streetlight and vanished into the night. That's all. Out of a lifetime, a few words, a few pictures, and everything you have lost is lurking there in the dark, poised to strike.

A PLACE FOR EVERYTHING

It's so easy to lose track of things. A screwdriver, for instance. "Where did I put that? I had it in my hand just a minute ago." You wander vaguely from room to room, having forgotten, by now, what you were looking for; staring into the refrigerator, the bathroom mirror … "I really could use a shave…."

Some objects seem to disappear immediately while others never want to leave. Here is a small black plastic gizmo with a serious demeanor that turns up regularly, like a politician at public functions. It seems to be an "integral part," a kind of switch with screw holes so that it can be attached to something larger. Nobody knows what. It probably went with something that was thrown away years ago. This thing's use has been forgotten, but it looks so important that we are afraid to throw it in the trash. It survives by bluff, like certain insects that escape being eaten because of their formidable appearance.

My father owned a large, three-bladed, brass propeller that he saved for years. Its worth was obvious, it was just that it lacked an immediate application since we didn't own a boat and lived hundreds of miles from any large bodies of water. The propeller survived all purges and cleanings, living, like royalty, a life of lonely privilege, mounted high on the garage wall.

HOW TO TELL A WOLF FROM A DOG

A wolf carries his head down, tail down. He has a look of preoccupation, or worry, you might think. He has a family to support. He probably has a couple of broken ribs from trying to bring down a moose, He's not getting workman's comp, either, and no praise for his efforts. The wolf looks unemployed, flat broke.

On the other hand, a dog of similar features, a husky or a malamute, has his head up, ears up, looks attentive, self-confident, cheerful and obedient. He is fully employed with an eye toward promotion. He carries his tail high, like a banner. He's part of a big organization and has the title of "man's best friend."

TIME MARCHES ON

How quickly the days are passing, Crazy Days, Wrong Days in Wright, Rutabaga Days, Duck Days, Red Flannel Days. Gone the Black fly Festival, the Eelpout Festival, Finn Fest, the Carnivore's Ball, the Five-Mile-Long Rummage Sale; all have passed. What has passed is forever lost. Modern Dance on the Bridge Abutment, the Hardanger Fiddle Association of America Meeting, the Polka Mass, "O, lost and by the wind grieved . . ." The Inline Skate Marathon, the Jet Ski Grand Prix . . . . What is past is as though it never was. The Battle of the Bands, the Polar Bear Plunge, the Monster Truck Challenge, the Poetry Slam . . .

SAINTHOOD

Because of my extraordinary correctness and sensitivity of late I have been elevated to the status of Temporary Minor Saint (secular). The position comes with a commendation praising my "uncharacteristic reticence tantamount to sagacity." This means that my entire being is now suffused with a pale radiance somewhat like the light from a small fluorescent bulb, the light on a kitchen range perhaps, only not quite so bright, and that instead of walking I now float at an altitude of approximately three inches above the ground. I move about at a slow and stately speed as befits my new rank. I move to the left or right by inclining my head and upper body in the appropriate direction. It's a less-than-perfect condition. The light keeps my wife awake at night and though the added height is beneficial, moving about in a crowd presents difficulties. My forward speed seems to be fixed and, though slow, is quite tricky to stop. I lean back but momentum carries me forward like a boat. Suddenly turning my head can send me veering into the person next to me or into a wall. In order to remain in one place I've found it necessary to attach cords to my belt on one end and to various solid objects around the room on the other. These days I take my meals standing up, tethered like the *Hindenburg*.

JANUARY

Daytime highs are well below zero. The air is absolutely clear and dry, the wind sharp, precise. We walk about in our bulky clothes like spacemen or old-fashioned divers on the bottom of the sea. The snow crunches underfoot. Now, above a single bare birch tree in the middle of a field of untrodden snow, the evening star appears in a most extraordinary blue sky. Everything is hard-edged, clear-cut. A perfect world made of glass. The sky is the exact color of Mary Beth Anderson's eyes. Beautiful, perfect. Perfect hair and perfect teeth. It always seemed that she knew exactly what she wanted and where she was going, that she had planned her life in detail. One thing I know for sure, she would have had no time for anyone who dresses the way we do.

THE TALK

He liked her immediately, her blue eyes, the way she listened, as if what he said was fascinating, the easy, natural way she laughed at all his jokes. Her rather conventional good looks and dress belied her intelligence. They had things in common, an interest in art and humanism. She talked about the problems of coffee growers in Central America. He listened but he also thought about kissing her on the neck, where her blond hair curled just behind her ear. He thought about other things, too. Mostly they laughed. Then she was silent. She looked at him. He saw that her eyes were gray, not blue. She was serious. She said, "Matt, this has gone too far in too short a time. I feel as though I'm being smothered. I have no time to myself anymore. I feel like you are always there. And I can't even so much as speak to another man . . ." "What are you talking about?" he said, "We only met an hour ago!" "That is exactly what I'm trying to say," she said.

IN A TAVERN

"It's no use," he says, "she's left me." This is after several drinks. It's as if he had said, "Van Gogh is my favorite painter." It's a cheap print he has added to his collection. He's been waiting all evening to show it to me. He doesn't see it. To him it's an incredible landscape, empty, a desert. "My life is empty." He likes the simplicity. "My life is empty. She won't come back." It is a landmark, like the blue mountains in the distance that never change. The crust of sand gives way with each step, tiny lizards skitter out of the way.... Even after walking all day there is no change in the horizon. "We're lost," he says. "No," I say, "let's go on." He says, "You go on. Take my canteen. You've got a reason to live." "No," I say, "we're in this together and we'll both make it out of here."

THE SNOWMAN
MONOLOGUES

I don't have the top hat like my ancestors . . . well, my predecessors, had. I've got a mad bomber hat. Quite trendy, I think. I've had to give up the pipe and I never drink. Still, I've got a big smile for everyone. I'm a traditionalist. I like the old songs, "White Christmas," "Ain't Misbehavin'," "Don't Get Around Much Anymore," songs like that. But I try to stay up-to-date. I'm very concerned about global warming, for instance, but it's difficult in my field to get any real information. And what can I do? Not that I'm complaining. I feel at home here, very much a part of my environment. It does get lonely at times though, there are so very few women in these parts and I'm not the best looking guy around, with my strange build and very odd nose. Sometimes I think they put my nose in the wrong place. Still, I have always hoped that someone would come along, someone who would melt in my arms, a woman with whom I could become one. You wouldn't guess it to look at me but I'm a romantic. But it's getting rather late in the season for me. So, I'm inclined just to drift.... I don't have any problems getting through the night; it's the days that are so long and difficult now that spring is coming. Oh, spring is beautiful with the new buds on the trees and the bright sunshine, but it's such a melancholy season. It causes one to reflect.... Oh, but here I go, running off at the mouth again.

BALONEY

There's a young couple in the parking lot, kissing. Not just kissing, they look as though they might eat each other up, kissing, nibbling, biting, mouths wide open, play fighting like young dogs, wrapped around each other like snakes. I remember that, sort of, that hunger, that passionate intensity. And I get a kind of nostalgic craving for it, in the way that I get a craving, occasionally, for the food of my childhood. Baloney on white bread, for instance: one slice of white bread with mustard or Miracle Whip or ketchup—not ketchup, one has to draw the line somewhere—and one slice of baloney. It had a nice symmetry to it, the circle of baloney on the rectangle of bread. Then you folded the bread and baloney in the middle and took a bite out of the very center of the folded side. When you unfolded the sandwich you had a hole, a circle in the center of the bread and baloney frame, a window, a porthole from which you could get a new view of the world.

BLUE, BLUE DAY

Some days are so sad nothing will help, when love has gone, when the sunshine and clear sky only tease and mock you. Those days you feel like running away, going where no one knows your name. Like slinging the old Gibson over your shoulder and traveling the narrow road to the North where the gray sky fits your mood and the cold wind blows a different kind of trouble. Nothing up there but mosquito-infested swamp, 10,000 acres of hummocky muck, a thicket of alder and dogwood, a twisted tangle of complications where not even Hemingway would fish. But somebody, someday soon, somebody will come and put up a bed and breakfast and a gourmet coffee shop. There is only one true wilderness left to explore, those vast empty spaces in your head.

BIG BROWN PILLS

I believe in the big brown pills: they lower cholesterol and improve digestion. They help prevent cancer and build brain cells. Plus, they just make you feel better overall. I believe in coffee and beet greens and fish oil, of course, and red wine, in moderation, and cinnamon. Green tea is good and black tea and ginseng. I eat my broccoli. Nuts are very good, and dark chocolate—has to be dark, not milk chocolate. Tomatoes. But I think the big brown pills really help. I used to believe in the little yellow pills, but now I believe in the big brown pills. I believe that they are much more effective. I still take the little yellow ones, but I really believe in the big brown ones.

BELIEF

We all have certain things we believe in. Usually they don't amount to much. Some people believe that if you put a spoon in the open bottle champagne will keep its fizz. Others believe that hot water will freeze faster than cold or that when you flush a toilet in the southern hemisphere the water always turns clockwise. Some people believe that you should wear a beanie and others believe in funny collars. In the absence of anything better these beliefs serve to separate your life from others lurking in the forest around you, like scent marking. People have certain phrases they like to use, also. At the end of the day … or … on the same page… and words such as paradigm, trope, facilitator, objecthood…. Words that don't mean anything. We drop them like breadcrumbs to mark the way home— where we all intend to return one day.

MY ANCESTRAL HOME

We came to a beautiful little farm. From photos I'd seen I knew this was the place. The house and barn were painted in the traditional Falu red, trimmed with white. It was nearly midsummer, the trees and grass, lush green. When we arrived the family was gathered at a table on the lawn for coffee and fresh strawberries. Introductions were made all around, Grandpa Sven, Lars-Olaf and Marie, Eric and Gudren, cousin Inge and her two children… It made me think of a Carl Larsen painting. But, of course, it was all modern, the Swedes are very up-to-date, Lars-Olaf was an engineer for Volvo, and they all spoke perfect English, except for Grandpa, and there was a great deal of laughter over my attempts at Swedish. We stayed for a long time laughing and talking, It was late in the day but the sun was still high. I felt a wonderful kinship. It seemed to me that I had known these people all my life, they even looked like family back in the States. But as it turned out we had come to the wrong farm. Lars-Olaf said, "I think I know your people, they live about three miles from here. If you like I could give them a call." I said that no, that it wasn't necessary, this was close enough.

TUMBLING TUMBLEWEEDS

Out on the Great Plains, where I was born, the wind blows constantly. When I was a kid I'd get 35 cents and run as hard as I could to the Lotta-Burger or the movie theatre only to find it had blown away. Going home was no better. Sometimes it would take a couple of days to find my house. Under these conditions it was impossible to get acquainted with the neighbors. It was a shock to open the front door and be faced with the county jail, the Pentecostal Church, or Aunt Erma carrying two large suitcases. Trash from all over the state caught and piled up at the edge of town, and during the windiest times of spring sometimes whole days blew away in a cloud of dust. I feel my natural lifespan may have been shortened by the experience. Still, it was a great place to grow up. As the old boy said, "You can have those big cities, people all jammed together. Give me some wide-open spaces." In the morning out on the plains you have a couple of cups of coffee, get all wound up and go like hell across an open field, try to bounce, clear both ditches and the highway so you don't get caught in the barbed wire, fly from one fenced-in nothing to another, hit the ground and keep on rolling.

GRAVITY

It turns out that the drain pipe from the sink is attached to nothing and water just runs right onto the ground in the crawl space underneath the house and then trickles out into the stream that passes through the back yard. It turns out that the house is not really attached to the ground but sits atop a few loose concrete blocks all held in place by gravity, which, as I understand it, means "seriousness." Well, this is serious enough. If you look into it further you will discover that the water is not attached to anything either, and that perhaps the rocks and the trees are not all that firmly in place. The world is a stage. But don't try to move anything. You might hurt yourself, besides that's a job for the stagehands and union rules are strict. You are merely a player about to deliver a soliloquy on the septic system to a couple dozen popple trees and a patch of pale blue sky.

FLORIDA

This morning at the university I passed a young woman in the hall that was wearing a very tight orange t-shirt with FLORIDA printed on the front in large white letters. Naturally I thought of citrus fruit. I thought of orange groves with workers tending the smudge pots on cold nights. I thought of Wallace Stevens in his white suit, walking barefoot on the beach, carrying his shoes with the socks tucked inside, and I imagined the moon over Miami. I have never been to Florida, but I know there are drug dealers, red tide, walking catfish, Republicans, Disney World, alligators, hanging chads…. Still, the citrus fruit is very good this time of year and when I peel an orange and look out the window at the snow and the rough spruce trees it seems like a miracle. One taste and I know there is a world beyond my imagining. It's impossible, like love, yet it really exists.

STARFISH

It seems like starfish don't do anything, but actually they move along at a rate of about 60 feet per hour. A starfish will eat anything that moves slower than it does, which excludes a great number of dishes from its diet. A starfish is all arms and appetite; it has no brain, yet in spite of this, time-lapse photography has shown that the starfish maintains an active social life. So in these regards the starfish is like many of the people you know.

MOCKINGBIRD

I remember when I was a child I had a pair of canaries in a cage in my bedroom. I had the idea that I would raise and sell canaries. I asked one of my sisters if she remembered them. She remembered that they were parakeets, not canaries. I asked another sister. She said she didn't remember any canaries but she remembered how mean I was to her. My youngest sister doesn't remember having birds but thinks that we had a pet rabbit. I don't remember that. My brother thinks we had a pet crow that talked. I don't remember a crow but I remember we had a myna bird for a while that said, "Hello sweetiepie," but he belonged to someone else. My mother says that she would never have allowed birds or any other animals in the house. I remember how the female canary ignored the male but chirped plaintively to a mockingbird that sang outside my window all summer long.

A HAPPY SONG

We know that birds' singing has to do with territory and breeding rights. Male birds sing to attract females and warn away other males. These songs include threat and intimidation, and perhaps, in the more complicated songs, the insinuation of legal action. It's the grim business of earning a living in a grim world. Each song has its own subtle sound, the idiosyncrasies of its singer. It turns out, though, that the females don't really value innovation and invention, and generally mate with males that sing the most ordinary, traditional tune. There is always though, some poor sap that doesn't get it, sitting alone on his branch practicing and polishing his peculiar version until it flows smoothly as water through the streambed, a happy song that fills us with joy on this first warm day of the year.

THE BIG BANG

When the morning comes that you don't wake up, what remains of your life goes on as some kind of electromagnetic energy. There's a slight chance you might appear on someone's screen as a dot. Face it. You are a blip or a ping, part of the background noise, the residue of the Big Bang. You remember the Big Bang, don't you? You were about 26 years old, driving a brand new red and white Chevy convertible, with that beautiful blond girl at your side. Charlene, was her name. You had a case of beer on ice in the back, cruising down Highway number 7 on a summer afternoon and then you parked near Loon Lake just as the moon began to rise. Way back then you said to yourself, "Boy, it doesn't get any better than this," and you were right.

SQUIRREL

The squirrel makes a split-second decision and acts on it immediately—headlong across the street as fast as he can go. Sure, it's fraught with danger, sure there's a car coming, sure it's reckless and totally unnecessary, but the squirrel is committed. He will stay the course.

APPARITION

She said "Take me to California. I want to see the ocean." As soon as I said yes I knew it was trouble. Right away I could see myself on the streets of Los Angeles without my wallet or maybe even without my pants. As it turned out I got no farther than Utah before I found myself hallooing into culvert openings. Now I've got myself into this and can't see a graceful way out. . . . The next morning bright as a penny, another sunny honeymoon on the dusty road, all on my own with the grasshoppers and the rattlesnakes, still a hundred miles from anywhere. She was beautiful and said all the silly things I wanted to hear. She said "Come with me and you can have your own life."

MARRIAGE

He said "People say marriage is like a three-legged race, but in our case she and I are tied together facing in the opposite directions on the stairs—she heading toward the main floor with the carpets and the furniture and such, and me heading to the basement with the furnace and the laundry tubs. It's okay, we get along, going nowhere, but it's damned difficult for the children or anyone else to get by us, whichever way they are headed."

A DISAPPOINTMENT

The best anyone can say about you is that you are a disappointment. We had higher expectations of you. We had hoped that you would finish your schooling. We had hoped that you would have kept your job at the plant. We had hoped that you would have been a better son and a better father. We hoped, and fully expected, that you would finish reading *Moby Dick*. I wish that, when I am talking to you, you would at least raise your head off your desk and look at me. There are people who, without your gifts, have accomplished so much in this life. I am truly disappointed. Your parents, your wife and children, your entire family, in fact, everyone you know is disappointed, deeply disappointed.

WISHES

Wishes, if they come true, always have a way of turning out badly. The fisherman's wife got wealth and power but wound up with nothing. Tithonus was given eternal life by Zeus but not eternal youth so the gift had unpleasant consequences. King Midas did not do well with his wish either. Solomon wished for wisdom, got wealth and power besides and still was not a happy man. Suppose you wished to be far away from the stupid, repressive town you grew up in and suddenly you were whirled away in a cloud of dust. Before long some well-intentioned fool would miss you and wish you home again. If you wished for a beautiful woman or rich and handsome husband you know what would happen. What is there to wish for finally? A blindfold and a last cigarette? No, we all know how bad smoking is for your health. When the genie comes out of the bottle or the man comes to your door with a check the size of a billboard you should say "No. No thank you." Say, "I don't want any." Say, "I wish you would go away." But you aren't going to, are you?

ICE

Walking on the icy pavement demands your attention. You have to learn to read the color, the texture, learn where you can safely step, learn to watch for the smooth, almost invisible ice or ice hidden by a light dusting of snow--suddenly you're flat on your back. Children don't worry about it. Their bodies are flexible and resilient and they have a shorter distance to fall. They fall, jump up and continue running. It's nothing. If a person of my age and size falls it makes a considerable impact. It's painful and embarrassing. Once I fell in front of the hardware store downtown, just like that, both feet straight out in front of me. Passersby gave me a strange look, not concern, more like disbelief. "What is this guy doing?" The very old, women on high-risk shopping trips, old men shoveling snow on rooftops, seem to have forgotten the ice entirely. If their frail bodies were caught by the least wind they would skitter and clatter over the hard surface for miles.

SOMERSAULT

Some children did handsprings or cartwheels. Those of us who were less athletically gifted did what we called somersaults, really a kind of forward roll. Head down in the summer grass, a push with the feet, then the world flipped upside-down and around. Your feet, which had been behind you, now stretched out in front. It was fun and we did it, laughing, again and again. Yet, as fun as it was, most of us, at some point, quit doing somersaults. But only recently, someone at Evening Rest (Managed Care for Seniors) discovered the potential value of somersaults as physical and emotional therapy for the aged, a recapturing of youth, perhaps. Every afternoon, weather permitting, the old people, despite their feeble protests, are led or wheeled onto the lawn, where each is personally and individually aided in the heels-over-head tumble into darkness. When the wind is right you can hear, even at this distance, the crying of those who have fallen and are unable to rise.

CONFESSIONAL POEM

I have this large tattoo on my chest. It is like a dream I have while I am awake. I see it in the mirror as I shave and brush my teeth, or when I change my shirt or make love. What can I do? I can't remember where I got the tattoo. When in the past did I live such a life? And the price of having such a large tattoo removed must be completely beyond reason. Still, the workmanship of the drawing is excellent, a landscape 8 x 10 inches in full color, showing cattle going downhill into a small western town. A young man, who might have been my great-grandfather, dressed as a cowboy and holding a rifle, stands at the top of the hill and points down toward the town. The caption beneath the picture reads: "Gosh, I didn't know we were this far west."

FISHERMAN: STONEY POINT

Here's an old guy talking to himself. He reels in his bait and says, "Son, you've got to go out there again. I know the rocks are treacherous, the water is deep. The winds can come up suddenly and there's no more than the thinnest line ties you to me. This is the way your life is going to be, out and back, again and again, partly in this world, partly in the other, never at home in either. Still, it's what you were born to do. You are young and strong, all steel and hooks. You know I'll do everything I can to bring you back safely. Go out there boy, and bring home a big fish for your old father to eat."

WHEN IT GETS COLD

When it gets cold around here we like to throw hot water into the air and watch it become instant ice mist that drifts away, never hitting the ground. Sometimes we drive nails with a frozen banana. Sometimes we just watch the numbers on the gas and the electric meters go spinning by. There's just no end to the fun.

But things get weird when it gets very cold. Things you never imagined come to life. There's an insect that appears, some kind of fly. Trees and houses make strange noises, and there are spooky, misty shapes moving around in the woods. Once when it was twenty-five below I found bare human footprints in snow that had fallen just a few hours before.

Everyone gets a little crazy when it's very cold for several weeks. Some people go in for compulsive house cleaning, others read, read everything: milk cartons, shipping labels.… We eat too much. We sleep a lot too. Once, during a cold spell, I slept for three days and when I woke I drank a gallon and a half of coffee.

WINTER CLOTHES

We come in puffing and stamping--goose down, wool, heavy boots, mittens, scarf. . . . Winter clothes bear the same relationship to the body as the body does to the soul, a sort of cocoon where those you thought you knew are changed beyond recognition. . . . We greet each other with awkward affection, like bears. Someone removes a glove and extends a pale hand.

His hand on the green silk of her dress, lightly, on the small of her back, sleepwalking there in the forest. And on the inside, the raveled thread ends, untidy windfall where the hunter walks to flush the startled bird . . . and afterwards silence . . . a handful of feathers, like letters from another woman found in a bank box after his death, casting a whole new light on the subject.

When you get to the end there is always one more thing. The mind insists that we live on after death whether we walk stiffly in bodies cold and drained of color or drift like tall columns of mist across the northern lakes, taller than we were in life but no more substantial.

We must look inside to find the answer, pulling the layers away like the leaves of an artichoke. And the answer is incorrect.

THE PREACHER

When times were hard, no work on the railroad, no work down on the farm, some of my ancestors took to preaching. It was not so much what was said as the way in which it was said. "The horn shall sound and the dog will bark and though you be on the highest mountain or down in the deepest valley when the darkness comes then you will lie down, and as the day follows the night you will surely rise again. The Lord our God hath made both heaven and earth. Oh, my dear brothers and sisters we know so well the ways of this world, think then what heaven must be like." It required a certain presence, a certain authority. The preacher was treated with respect and kept at a bit of a distance, like a rattler. There wasn't much money in it but it was good for maybe a dozen eggs or a chicken dinner now and then.

HOCKEY

Ice hockey makes very little sense to the innocent bystander. Yet people in this area are passionate about the sport, so, like religion and politics, it is a subject best not brought up in polite conversation. The players, with their skates and heavily padded uniforms (which for some strange reason include shorts) all trying to whack the puck into one or the other of the nets, seems, to the uninitiated viewer, a very approximate operation, something like trying to knit while wearing boxing gloves. One of the biggest problems for the spectator and, evidently, for the players as well, is that the puck is hard to see. It is so small and shoots across the ice at great speed or gets caught beneath a mass of fallen players. This causes a great deal of frustration among the players, which they vent upon one another. Long ago, before we became so politically correct, hockey was played using a recently detached human head as a puck. More brutal perhaps, but much easier to follow the puck.

FREYA GOES SHOPPING

Nobody thinks about how difficult it is to embody all beauty, sexual desire, hope, love, domestic bliss and wild runaway passion; in short to represent some wide-ranging, out of control, hormonal brush fire. Everyone thinks *what a great job.* But no one understands what it means to be a symbol, a deity. It's way worse than being merely a queen, or a movie star, I can tell you. My own feelings are never considered. I have no private life. I'm too busy being some kind of universal principle. No one wonders if this is what I really want, if this is right for me. Well, come Friday I'm taking off. I'm going to have some quality time: my time, my place, my self. I may do some shopping at *The Dwarves.* They have some beautiful things. They have a necklace down there made of rubies and amber that is to die for. And it would go so nicely with that earth-red shawl I have. They have an outrageous price on that necklace, but I know those guys and I know what they want.

INSECTS

Insects never worry about where they are. A mosquito is so dedicated to the pursuit of warm blood that it neglects the long-range plan. If a mosquito follows you into the house it waits patiently until the lights are out and you are nearly asleep. Then it heads straight for your ear. Suppose you miss, hit yourself in the head and knock yourself out and the mosquito succeeds in drawing blood. How will it get out of the house again to breed? What are its chances?

Insects don't seem to have a sense of place but require only a certain ambiance. A fly that gets driven 500 miles in a car and then is finally chased out the window does not miss the town where it spent its maggothood. Wherever this is it will be the same; a pile of dog shit, a tuna salad sandwich, a corpse.

EARL

In Sitka, because they are fond of them, people have
named the sea lions. Every sea lion is named Earl
because they are killed one after another by the orca,
the killer whale; sea lion bodies tossed left and right
into the air. "At least he didn't get Earl," someone says.
And sure enough, after a time, that same friendly,
bewhiskered face bobs to the surface. It's Earl again.
Well, how else are you to live except by denial, by
some palatable fiction, some little song to sing while
the inevitable, the black and white blindsiding fact,
comes hurtling toward you out of the deep?

NAPPING NEAR THE SUCKER RIVER

The stream goes on and on, babbling and blathering about something, something it knows nothing about. It is like listening from your bed as a child to the ha-ha mumble murmur of adults in the other room. If you listen the way you did then, the river as well will put you to sleep. The river says, "... everything goes down, down, soon everything that happened will not have happened it has been a very long time since you checked the oil in your car a long time since you called your mother everything you used think was important wasn't important what you were told was important wasn't what you think is important now isn't important only what you think is unimportant only what you did not even think of only what you could never think of could never imagine is important... but not very important...."

WALKING THROUGH A WALL

Unlike flying or astral projection, walking through walls is a totally earth-related craft, but a lot more interesting than pot making or driftwood lamps. I got started at a picnic up in Bowstring in the northern part of the state. A fellow walked through a brick wall right there in the park. I said, "Say, I want to try that." Stone walls are best, then brick and wood. Wooden walls with fiberglass insulation and steel doors aren't so good. They won't hurt you. If your wall walking is done properly, both you and the wall are left intact. It is just that they aren't pleasant somehow. The worst things are wire fences, maybe it's the molecular structure of the alloy or just the amount of give in a fence, I don't know, but I've torn my jacket and lost my hat in a lot of fences. The best approach to a wall is, first, two hands placed flat against the surface; it's a matter of concentration and just the right pressure. You will feel the dry, cool inner wall with your fingers, then there is a moment of total darkness before you step through on the other side.

FISH OUT OF WATER

When he finally landed the fish it seemed so strange, so unlike other fishes he'd caught, so much bigger, more silvery, more important, that he half expected it to talk, to grant his wishes if he returned it to the water. But the fish said nothing, made no pleas, gave no promises. His fishing partner said, "Nice fish. You ought to have it mounted." Other people who saw it said the same thing, "Nice fish…." So he took it to the taxidermy shop but when it came back it didn't look quite the same. Still, it was an impressive trophy. Mounted on a big board the way it was, it was too big to fit in the car. In those days he could fit everything he owned into the back of his Volkswagen. But the fish changed all that. After he married, a year or so later, nothing would fit in the car. He got a bigger car. Then a new job, children…. The fish moved with them from house to house, state to state. All that moving around took its toll on the fish, it began to look worn, a fin was broken off. It went into the attic of the new house. Just before the divorce became final, when he was moving to an apartment, his wife said, "Take your goddamn fish." He hung the fish on the wall before he'd unpacked anything else. The fish seemed huge, too big for this little apartment. Boy, it was big. He couldn't imagine he'd ever caught a fish that big.

JACKSTRAW

You look for deeper meanings in things. There are signs and portents, though sometimes you deny it. You find special significance in certain places and days, the cottage by the lake, Christmas, a certain Chinese restaurant in Winnipeg, your birthday, and set them up like signposts marking the passage of your life. One after another they multiply until you're surrounded by a forest of sticks. Jackstraws. Touch one and they all fall down. Jack Straw, head full of hay, reading long boring books, waiting for the mail, watching the days go by. Here it is Sunday morning and there's no one downtown but the looney and dysfunctional. There's old One-Eye who recently returned from Jupiter, and the spooky Woman in White, Tom Drooley, Mr. Ozone Peepot, Euclid and The Motorcycle Queen, Mr. Occupant, Goofy Walker, Old Man Winter, still wearing his down parka. It's spring. It's April Fools. It's the Easter parade! Grab your hat and let's get in line!

THE SPEAKER

The speaker points out that we don't really have much of a grasp of things, not only the big things, the important questions, but the small everyday things. "How many steps up to your front door? What kind of tree grows in your back yard? What is the name of your district representative? What is your wife's shoe size? Can you tell me the color of your sweetheart's eyes? Do you remember where you parked the car?" The evidence is overwhelming. Most of us never truly experience life. "We drift through life in a daydream, missing the true richness and joy that life has to offer." When the speaker has finished we gather around to sing a few inspirational songs. You and I stand at the back of the group and hum along since we have forgotten most of the words.

THE AFTERLIFE

Older people are exiting this life as if it were a movie…
"I didn't get it," they are saying.
He says, "It didn't seem to have any plot."
"No." she says, "it seemed like things just kept coming at me. Most of the time I was confused … and there was way too much sex and violence."
"Violence anyway," he says.
"It was not much for character development either; most of the time people were either shouting or mumbling. Then just when someone started to make sense and I got interested, they died. Then a whole lot of new characters came along and I couldn't tell who was who."
"The whole thing lacked subtlety."
"Some of the scenery was nice."
"Yes."
They walk on in silence for a while. It is a summer night and they walk slowly, stopping now and then, as if they had no particular place to go. They walk past a streetlamp where some insects are hurling themselves at the light, and then on down the block, fading into the darkness.
She says, "I was never happy with the way I looked."
"The lighting was bad and I was no good at dialogue," he says.
"I would have liked to have been a little taller," she says.

INDEX

After forty or more winters in Duluth, Minnesota, Louis Jenkins now runs away when snow begins to fall, to the Southwest where he continues to write prose poems, despite good advice. He has also written, along with Mark Rylance, actor and former director of the Globe Theatre, London, a stage production titled *Nice Fish* based on Jenkins poems. The play premiered at the Guthrie Theater, Minneapolis, in April, 2013.